D1451485

MIECZKONSH

WHAT WE CAN DO ABOUT

RECYCLING GARBAGE

Donna Bailey

Franklin Watts

New York   London   Toronto   Sydney

Franklin Watts
387 Park Avenue South
New York, NY 10016

Design: Julian Holland Publishing Ltd.
Illustrator: Martin Smillie
Picture Research: Alison Renwick
Printed in Italy

Library of Congress Cataloging-in-Publication Data
Bailey, Donna.
  Recycling garbage/Donna Bailey.
    p. cm. — (What we can do about)
  Includes index.
  Summary: Discusses how various waste materials are recycled and proposes ways
for children to act more responsibly toward the environment.
  ISBN 0-531-11017-6
  1. Recycling (Waste, etc.) — Juvenile literature. 2. Environmental protection —
Citizen participation — Juvenile literature.
  [1. Recycling (Waste). 2. Environmental protection — Citizen participation.
3. Refuse and refuse disposal.] I. Title. II. Series.
TD794.5.B35   1991
363.72'82 — dc20   90-13103
                                                                      CIP
                                                                       AC

Photograph acknowledgements
t = top b = bottom
Cover: Chris Fairclough Colour Library
pp3 Alcan Aluminum Ltd, 6 Chris Fairclough Colour Library, 7 David Goulston/
Bruce Coleman Ltd, 8 R Dorel/Robert Harding Picture Library, 9 t Chris
Fairclough Colour Library, 9b Ian Griffiths/Robert Harding Picture Library, 10
Jimmy Holmes/The Environmental Picture Library, 11 Chris Fairclough Colour
Library, 12 Jimmy Holmes/The Environmental Picture Library, 13t Jack Dermid/
Bruce Coleman Ltd, 13b Philip Carr/The Environmental Picture Library, 14 Jimmy
Holmes/The Environmental Picture Library, 15 S & R Greenhill, 16 Alcan
Aluminum Ltd, 17 Warren Spring Laboratory, 18 C B & D W Frith/Bruce Coleman
Ltd, 19t John Lythgage/Planet Earth Pictures, 19b Mark Boulton/ICCE
Photolibrary, 20, 21, 22, 23t, 23b Chris Fairclough Colour Library, 24 Alex
Williams/Greenpeace Communications Ltd, 25 Barry Waddams, 26 Chris
Fairclough Colour Library, 27 Topham Picture Source.

Contents

Too much garbage

Have you ever looked inside your garbage can? Most of our garbage is a mixture of many different kinds of things. There may be glass bottles, plastic bottles, plastic bags, newspapers, tin cans and vegetable peels.

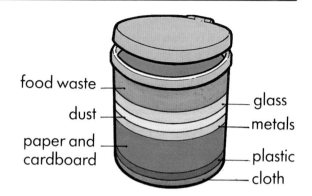

food waste
dust
paper and cardboard
glass
metals
plastic
cloth

The average amounts of different materials in a typical garbage can.

Every year, each household throws away about one **ton** of garbage. If you think how many **households** there are in the country and add together all their garbage, it comes to a huge amount. Then there is the waste from factories, stores, restaurants and farms. We have to get rid of all this garbage somehow.

Most household garbage is dumped in large holes, such as old **quarries**. Some garbage is burned. Both these ways of getting rid of garbage can cause problems such as **pollution**. It would be less wasteful if we could reuse garbage or make new things from it. This is known as **recycling**.

Bury it or burn it?

In most towns and cities, we put our garbage into lidded waste containers. These containers are placed near the curb on certain days of the week when they are then emptied into large sanitation trucks.

Inside the trucks the garbage is squashed to take up as little space as possible. The garbage is then taken to a garbage dump, or **landfill site**. As suitable sites near the towns fill up, the garbage trucks must travel longer distances to the landfill site. This in turn results in higher costs because more gasoline is needed to run the trucks and it takes longer to deliver the garbage to the landfill site.

At the landfill site the garbage is flattened by bulldozers. Then heavy **compactors** with spiked wheels, like the one in the picture, squash the garbage even more. At the end of every day the garbage is covered with a layer of earth to stop rats and flies getting into the waste.

Landfill sites have other problems. Water from rain or underground streams draining through the sites may mix with the poisonous liquids which are made as the garbage breaks down. When this polluted water drains into streams and ponds it can harm wildlife.

Sometimes, instead of being buried, garbage is burned in large machines called **incinerators**. Huge magnets pick out any steel, tin or pieces of iron. These can be recycled. The rest of the garbage is burned to ash. The ash takes up only about 10 percent of the space of the original garbage. The ash can be used for making roads.

It is often better to burn garbage than to bury it, but burning has its problems, too. Incineration produces harmful gases and solids that pollute the air. Today there are strict rules about how garbage should be burned in incinerators.

Why not recycle it?

When you think about the huge amounts of garbage we produce and the problems that can occur when we try to bury or burn it, it makes sense to reuse or recycle what we can. About 75 percent of the garbage produced could be reused or recycled.

In many parts of the world, people do not throw away so much garbage. The people in countries such as India and China are more likely to try to reuse or recycle things.

These workers in Pakistan have found many different ways of using old rubber tires. They turn the worn-out tires into rubber buckets, and rubber soles for shoes.

Recycling means making new goods from things that have been used and are not needed any more. The old newspapers in the picture can be broken down into a **pulp** and made into new paper goods such as cardboard and egg cartons. Glass jars can be melted down and made into new glassware. Food scraps and vegetable and fruit peels can be made into **compost** to spread on the soil in the garden. Only plastics are difficult to recycle at the moment because there are so many different kinds.

Sorting for recycling

Different kinds of garbage are recycled in different ways. This means that garbage must be sorted into different kinds of materials, such as metal, glass, paper, old clothes, and plant waste.

In China, bottles are carefully sorted and put into wire baskets. Cardboard is folded flat and tied up in bundles ready for collection. This makes it much easier to collect the bottles and cardboard for recycling, especially when the garbage is taken away on a bicycle.

Metals

Metal food and drink cans are probably made of either **steel** or **aluminum**. The two metals can be separated at home by a simple test. Put a magnet on the side of a can. If it falls off, the can is aluminum, which is not magnetic. The magnet will cling to a steel can.

It is easy to recycle aluminum. In the United States, 60 percent of aluminum drink cans are recycled. People sell huge sacks of aluminum cans to buyers who call regularly at convenient collecting points, like shopping malls. Steel can be recycled and made into new cars, stoves and refrigerators.

Glass

Glass bottles and jars must be sorted by color before they are recycled. Any tops should be removed first. **Bottle banks** and **recycling centers** have separate containers to help people sort out the different colors. The broken glass, or **cullet**, of each color is melted down separately to make new glass of that color.

Paper

Wastepaper can be mixed with water and broken down by machine into pulp. This is similar to the wood pulp which is made from crushing trees. The pulp from wastepaper is very often used to make cardboard. Our picture shows cardboard being made from recycled paper. The cardboard sheets are drying in the sun.

Old clothes

Good quality used clothes and blankets are always wanted by charities such as the Salvation Army. If the clothes are clean and in good condition, they can be sold to raise funds for the charity.

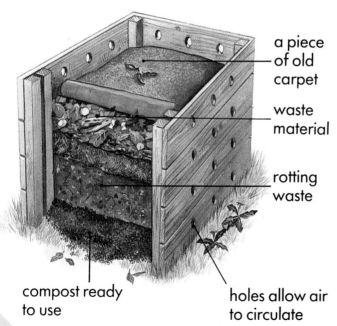

a piece of old carpet

waste material

rotting waste

compost ready to use

holes allow air to circulate

Plant waste

Quite a lot of garbage from the kitchen is made of plant material. Cabbages and other vegetables usually need to have some of their outer leaves cut off before they are cooked. Banana and other fruit skins are put in the garbage. This kind of garbage can easily be collected in a separate container and then be used to make compost. When all the vegetable remains have been broken down, the compost can be put on the soil to help plants grow well. Most cuttings from the garden can also be made into compost.

Plastics

In some places, plastics are collected for recycling. It is not easy to recycle plastics because the different kinds of plastic must first be sorted out. Mixed plastic cannot be used for recycling.

In Germany and some parts of the United States, you pay a **deposit** when you buy a full plastic bottle. When you take your empty plastic bottle back to the store, you get the deposit back. This encourages people to return their empty plastic bottles and not just throw them away. The stores then return the bottles to the company that made them for refilling or recycling.

Recycling and energy

When goods are made in a factory, **energy** is needed to make machines work. Coal and oil are used to make heat energy and to make electricity in power stations.

Heat energy may be used to separate metals from their **ores**. The metals are used to make different kinds of goods. Electrical energy is needed to drive machines in factories. It generally takes less energy to make goods from recycled materials than to use **raw materials**.

It takes about twice as much energy to make paper from wood pulp as it takes to make recycled paper. Making aluminum from used drinks cans, like the ones in the photograph, takes only 5 percent of the energy needed to extract aluminum from its ore.

Garbage can be used to produce heat energy. **Methane** gas given off from garbage in landfill sites can be burned to produce heat energy. This energy can be used for warming homes and for making electricity.

Household waste can also be turned into **refuse derived fuel**, or **RDF**. This is made by cutting and crushing the garbage into small pieces or pellets, like the ones in the photograph. The pellets can then be burned to produce heat.

Heat from modern incinerators can be used to warm water and to produce energy to drive machines. All the garbage collected in Disneyland in California is burned in an incinerator and the heat is used to make electricity. Denmark uses about 30 percent of its household waste in this way to produce energy.

Recycling and the environment

Recycling garbage is usually better for the environment than making goods from raw materials. The main ore used to make aluminum is bauxite. Most bauxite comes from tropical countries, where it is dug out of large surface mines. These mines destroy an enormous amount of land and look very ugly. It is easy to recycle aluminum. Recycling more aluminum would mean fewer bauxite mines and less destruction of the environment.

It takes about 17 trees to make one ton of paper. Large areas of land are needed to grow trees for the huge amount of paper we use. Many people think that the **plantations** where the trees are grown do not look attractive because only one type of tree is planted. It is more interesting to see a variety of trees. The plantations also take up land that could be used for farming. If we recycle more paper we would need fewer plantations.

Power stations that burn oil or coal pollute the air with heavy smoke and fumes. These fumes mix with water vapor in the air to make acid rain.

In Germany and the United States, oil extracted from old worn-out rubber tires is used as a fuel in some power stations. This kind of fuel causes less air pollution than burning coal.

What can you do?

Reduce your garbage

Goods in stores often have lots of separate wrappings. Chocolates may each be wrapped inside a box which is covered by a layer of plastic. When you buy the chocolates, the store clerk usually puts them in a bag. Try to buy goods with as little wrapping as possible. The wrapping and bag not only add to the cost of the goods, but usually go straight into the garbage can.

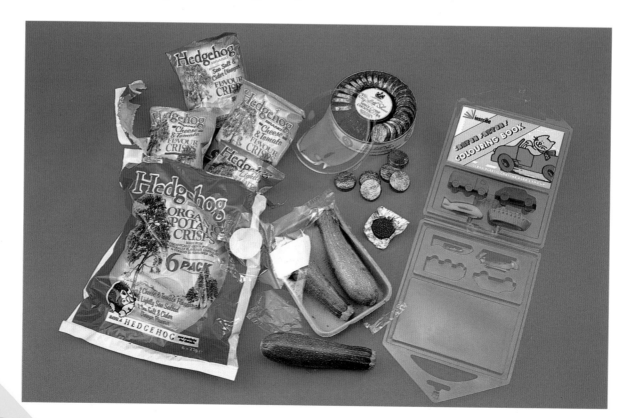

Another way to avoid instant garbage is not to accept leaflets handed out in the street, or plastic bags provided free in supermarkets. Take your own bag when you go shopping and use it instead.

Today many goods are designed to be **disposable** and are meant to be used only once. Disposable diapers and disposable plates and glasses may be more convenient and save time, but they create yet more garbage.

Whenever you can, buy good quality goods that will last longer. A well-made toy is more likely to survive and be passed on to another child, than a poorly-made toy which will soon get broken and end up in the garbage.

Reuse your garbage

Some things, like plastic containers and glass jars, can easily be reused as long as they are not damaged and are made really clean. Many plastic bags can be reused, and most cardboard boxes as well. Wherever possible buy goods in reusable containers.

Try to think of other uses for things you have finished with. A large cardboard box could be used as a playhouse for a younger brother or sister. Plastic yogurt and margarine containers make good pots for growing small plants. You can probably come up with lots of other good ideas.

If you or your family have no way of reusing something, someone else may be grateful for it. Clothes and toys that you have grown out of but not worn out can be given to thrift shops or tag sales.

Recycle your garbage

If you cannot reuse something, at least try to recycle it. If your garbage for recycling is not collected separately, find out whether there is a recycling center nearby. Your local supermarket parking lot may have a bottle bank where you can leave glass bottles and jars for recycling.

Whenever you can, buy things that are made from recycled materials. If people buy more recycled goods, firms will be more eager to make them. When you are using something that is recycled, encourage your friends to do the same.

Setting a good example

When you wonder what to do about your garbage remember the three Rs: REDUCE, RECYCLE, REUSE. Try not to create so much garbage in the first place. If you have something you no longer need, think about whether you can reuse it. If not, could it be recycled? Do not throw away anything until you are sure you cannot reuse or recycle it.

Some countries have laws about sorting out garbage to encourage recycling. Some **municipal authorities** have door-to-door collection programs for different kinds of garbage.

REDUCE

RECYCLE   REUSE

People in the United States and some European countries are given a different color of bin, or sometimes several different colored bins, to sort their garbage into. The sorted garbage is collected by special garbage trucks with separate compartments for the various kinds of garbage. Sometimes each type of garbage is collected on a different day. In Oregon, if you do not sort your waste it will not be picked up!

In France, most supermarkets sell drinks in glass bottles that can be returned for refilling. In West Germany and the Netherlands, bottles for drinks are all made the same shape and size, whatever the contents. This makes reuse much easier. Shoppers take their cartons of empty bottles back to the supermarket. The supermarkets then return the bottles to the **manufacturers** for refilling.

In Germany the government uses recycled paper to make some school books. As well as setting a good example, the off-white/gray paper makes people realize that good paper need not be white.

Activities

1 Make a survey of how many cans of soft drinks your friends drink each week. What do they do with the empty cans? Do they recycle them? If not, use the information you have collected to design a poster to encourage them to do so.

2 Ask your teacher to help you to organize a recycling exhibition at your school. Collect as many things as you can that have been made from recycled materials. The picture shows some recycled goods. How many others can you find?

3 Make a chart with these headings:

Newspapers and magazines
Other paper and cardboard
Glass bottles and jars
Plastic bottles and jars
Plastic wrappings and bags
Metal cans
Vegetable and fruit peelings
Other food scraps

Ask your family to keep a record of all the things they throw away in one week. Every time they put something in the garbage, they should mark it on your chart. At the end of the week, ask them to see if they can reduce the amount a little next week.

Glossary

aluminum: a light, strong metal used to make many containers.

bottle bank: a container where empty glass bottles and jars can be left for recycling.

compactor: a machine that crushes things so that they take up less space.

compost: waste from leaves, grass cuttings, and vegetable peels broken down to make food for growing plants.

cullet: broken bits of glass used in the glassmaking process.

deposit: a small amount of money paid on something. The money is returned later if, for example, the bottle or container is returned to the store.

disposable: made in order to be used once and then thrown away.

energy: the fuel necessary for work. People need food for energy. Machines need a fuel like electricity or gasoline.

household: a family or group of friends who share the same house.

incinerator: a machine for burning garbage.

landfill sites: large holes in the ground where garbage is dumped and buried.

manufacturer: a company that makes goods.

methane: a gas that is given off when garbage breaks down.

ore: a rock or mineral from which a useful metal can be obtained.

plantation: an area where a lot of trees of the same kind are being grown.

pollution: something which dirties or poisons the air, land, or water.

pulp: a wet, soft, mushy substance made from very small pieces of wood or paper and water.

quarry: a place where rocks and minerals are dug out of the ground.

raw materials: natural substances which are grown or taken out of the ground.

recycle: to make something new from something already used once.

recycling center: a place where you can take materials such as paper, glass, cans, plastic and old clothes and put them into containers so that they can be recycled.

refuse derived fuel (RDF): small lumps of crushed garbage that can be burned to produce heat.

steel: a hard metal used to make knives, tools, machinery and containers.

ton: a measurement of weight, equal to 2,000 lb.

Index